Listen

Poetry by

Claire Conroy

Copyright © 2018 Claire Conroy

All rights reserved.

ISBN: 978-0-692-04312-7

Library of Congress Control Number: 2018912175

Front & back cover art by Claire Conroy

Printed by DiggyPOD, Inc., in the United States of America.

First Printing 2018

DiggyPOD, Inc

301 Industrial Drive

Tecumseh, MI 49286

Listen

Poetry by

Claire Conroy

~CONTENTS~

1- Listen	9
2- Sweet Friend	11
3- The State of Green Mountains	13
4- Gypsy Girl	15
5- Hanging Around for You	19
6- Market Square	21
7- Journey of Embryo	23
8- Terms and Conditions May Apply	25
9- Phantoms	27
10- Master of Monticello	29
11- Pagan Prayer	33
12- Paint Me	35
13- I See You in Malibu	39
14- The Moon is a Harlot	41
15- The Duke	45
16- M.E.W. (Mistrust in the Eyes of a Woman)	47
17- Caffe Kilim	49
18- Alexandria: Hypatia's Passion	51
19- Linger with Me	53
20- Love for Joni's Palette	55

~CONTENTS~

21- Orion	57
22- Ballad of Anne Boleyn (part 1)	59
23- Ballad of Anne Boleyn (part 2)	61
24- Daybreak	63
25- Naughty Nymphs	65
26- Earthly Delights in the Dirt	67
27- All Cycle and Dance	69
28- Merely a Meal	71
29- Sown Seeds of Scion	73
30- Early Autumn Came the Fall	75
31- For Us (part 1)	77
32- For Us (part 2)	79
33- Curtains	81
34- Cold Sun	83
35- Only in These Short Hours	87
36- Seacoast Salutes Spring	89
37- Zenith of Mr. Frost	91
38- Chase Me to Paris	93
39- Centaurs and Metaphors	95
40- Oyster River	97
About the Author	99

Dedication

I would like to dedicate this book to my amazing daughter, Montana West. This is for you, my sweet one...do what makes you happy. Don't be afraid to share your joy and know I love you fiercely.

A very big thank you to my Dad, Lawrence Conroy. Even if my choices were questionable, you have always had my back & supported my decisions. Completely unconditionally. I love and respect you to no end. I could not have written this book without you

Always remember the meaning of life, friends.
We are only here to help one another.
Find happiness in this and you will be truly blessed.
So Mote it Be.

Make good choices!

Much love,
Claire Marie Conroy

Listen

Respect my changes,
For I feel they are good.
Try my advice,
Because maybe you should.

Don't doubt my opinions,
For they are how I feel.
Don't open old wounds,
Because once they were real.

Listen to music,
For there's meaning in song.
Forgive me for yesterday,
Because then I was wrong.

Don't say "I once loved you",
For that love wasn't true.
Please listen to me,
Because I listen to you.

Sweet Friend

This river of yours,
New to you, newer still to me,
Is rushing past us now,
While you rest.

Green retreat of lush mountain roads
Leading toward a quaint space.
River rolling alongside
Your cabin of sweet solitude.

Enchantment.
Flower-clad nymphs also reside
With you here.
Their giggles stifled by the river.

I send blessings to you,
My dear, green sister in the wood.
And know you are indeed
In the place where your heart will go.

The State of Green Mountains

Magic rests easy there.
Alabaster fields where seeds sleep,
Rivers rife with glittering ice.
Woodlands laden, snow so deep.

Wakes slow, springtime thawing
Finds sprite-like enthusiasm in mud.
Whispered promises tell
Of flowers from spellbound bud.

Summer assaulted by sorcery.
Mountains fresh green revived,
Lake deep beckons prophecy,
Secrets rain like tears cried.

Autumn wears a crown of jinx.
Foliage filled with faeries charm,
Alchemy covered skies where
A covenant of snowflakes swarm.

Vermont, I love you.

Gypsy Girl

Keep walking.
The caravan left you behind long ago.
Pay no heed
To those minstrels.

They play pretty sonnets
To warm the cold resolve.
Loosen the locket
Protecting your beaten heart.

Sadist ruffians cannibalized your love.
Left just enough
To grow back,
Only to be dined upon by brothers.

You've grown, Gypsy Girl.
Shake ribbons & charms from your pockets.
Take up your card of destiny
And play it.

This is your hand.
No thief or prince can deal
A game of solitaire
Of tarot to foretell.

Slow down, whirling dervish.
Your sovereign nomad awaits,
Too patient in lust;
Your dust will cloak and veil him.

Bohemia lays before you,
He is there.
Take time on this journey,
Let this noble man discover you.

Refugee find sanctuary,
Country and time; for now
A Gypsy Girl stands
By your side.

Hanging Around for You

I don't dare apologize
For my weakened spirit,
Or excuse my blue mood.
Letting my inner human
Through the facade I front.

Draw the curtain closed
On my world,
Then shed my skin.
Begin to wrestle myself,
My deeds against my sins.

This karmic wheel is swift,
Perpetual turning.
Giving great flow
Into sudden halt.
The torture of grinding pause.

Time is punishment
In times like these.
Noose-like patience
Where I find myself
Hanging around for you.

What penance do I pay?
Here and now, where
I cannot seem to find you.
Further sacrifice required
When years of bondage bleed.

Market Square

In the old port town
Of my birth and blood,
Endured the trial of youth
Fledgling tears, a flood.

Coffee fueled daylight
Confused evening's slowed pace.
No connections, all acquaintance
Shallow dancers left no trace.

My antiquated hamlet,
Handsome Market Square.
Hub of downtown's history,
One spring I met you there.

Affections, to the heart of me.
Sweet lies, your arrow struck.
I fell a victim to not knowing
You didn't give a fuck.

Pin holed perception of
This small-town minded girl,
Thrown headlong down your rabbit hole,
Ribbons tattered, they unfurl.

Frivolous green desire
Grows bitter fruit on the vine.
Time ripened love to harvest
And healed this heart of mine.

Journey of Embryo

Lovely melodic twangs
Sing a ramble down the line.
Stumbling smile and stride,
Hide and seek with sidewalk shadow.
Thumbing, bumming a ride.
Country miles, just going.
Strumming, humming a happy diddy.
Jorma making time,
Confounding reason and rhyme.
Lighthearted man rolling
Cajoling charity from strangers
To hear his joyous tune.
Caroling liberty filled notes
From a tired guitar.
He doesn't even want
A spot in your backseat.
Road weary sounds need an ear,
It's modest, lively and clear,
Rooted in jovial reflection.
Highway kindness is bleak
For those who seek
To know more than the feeling
Of this traveling song.

Terms and Conditions May Apply

"Satisfaction guaranteed!
Terms and Conditions May Apply"
Should be tattooed
Below your belly button.
Warning potential trespassers
The dangers that lay in your pleasures.
The dark, beautiful place
In your eyes
That is liable to open up and swallow
The innocent
Whole.

Phantoms

Bathroom mirror
In its aging state,
Carries ghosts
Lingering on its glass.

The ring on my finger,
Bejeweled by the stone
Of my birth, once gleamed;
Now softened with wear.

Garnet-like wine
Seems grey
Seen through the antique goblet
He gave me so long ago.

Morning sunlight blinds me,
Although I washed the windshield
Inside and out
Just the night before.

My spectacles fail me.
These clouds...phantoms
Refuse my attentions
And stay on the lens.

Or is it my own mind
Denying my sight,
Burdened
By specters I won't see?

Master of Monticello

Assigned a task
Write words that last
And cling to minds of men.
This shy, mild spoken agrarian
Retired privately with ink
And captured rights of liberty
For the American.
Voicing independence desired,
This hypocrite, duality
Found plainly in his deeds.
Holding leashes on lives,
Handing lashes to taskmasters
While shouting "Freedom!" on paper.
Saluting thoughts of being judged
Solely on merit,
Not of birth or station
But on your integrity, yet
Holding the flesh of slaves.
Imprinted seed in this soil.
Mourning loss of honored wife
While siring bastards.
Future and humanity,
These passions drove politics.
Religion to be freed
Under Statutes of Virginia.
Expansion for the people
Through paths of Lewis and Clark.
The banned importation
Of African bodies,
Never unchaining those he bound.
What a paradoxical president.
One who shrugged the title,
Never returning to the Capitol.

Architect of little mountain,
Aggressive scientist of soil.
Philosopher forms atheneum
To sell every book
From sheer necessity,
Only to foster our
Library of Congress.
Founding Father wielding pen
With co-scribe Adams.
Brotherly friendship
Upon opposite sides of scales.
Extraordinary fate these two,
Fifty years on the day
When nation celebrated
What they declared.
To see the day, then depart.
What is this man
But an American enigma?

Pagan Prayer

Blessed Be are we!~
Bathed in the Sun once more.
Baptized in illumination.
Washed with day.
Blessed Be are we!~
Barefoot upon dirt.
Hands in the soil.
Worshipping ground, Earth.
Blessed Be are we!~
Wind-kissed wild-eyed beings.
Breath cleansed by holy zephyrs,
Blown through lovely life, Air.
Blessed Be are we!~
Kindle kindness alight
In the heart of simple beings
Burning with zest, Fire.
Blessed Be are we!~
Pulsing vein-like rivers.
Rains render us clean.
Great life blood, Water.
Blessed Be are we!~
To be moved so by Moon.
Moody sphere, then shards,
Gathered nightly and revered.

Blessed Be are we!~
Soul aroused by Spirit.
Attraction of solar dust.
We are but stars.

Paint Me

A mysterious artist loved so deeply
For a woman,
He secretly made a paintbrush
From a lock of her hair.

She gave this to him
Freely, and with her love.

He walked deeply into woods
Alone, in solitude, in thought,
In her, and for her gathered
Those thoughts.

Having no knowing
Of her unyielding ache to be known.

She had been waiting.
Hope drowning her fear,
"He WILL return to me …
I beg it of him…"

And from longing into dream.
Waiting.

Restlessness, a stirring
Roused the muse from slumber
To find her lost lover,
Her painter, come home.

"This is how I need to love you."
He placed the canvas on the easel.
Laying out paint lovingly
Upon the palette;
He placed her on the bed
Just as sweetly.

"Paint me." She spoke
With a need that he recognized.

Stirring the movement
In his heart to guide his hand,
Took up the paintbrush
She did not know existed.

Gently dabbing the dye
Well acquainted with where it needed to go.

His hands having known
The strokes the paint brush
Wanted to caress;
Canvas is as her curves.

"I cannot hold you, you're sand.
I can only hope to remember your softness like this."

She lay supine, open, exposed
But still felt he could not see the depth
True and unwavering devotion
Of her love that existed. ...

...Then I pull myself reluctantly from this waking dream of mine.
Only to wish you felt for me as he.

I See You in Malibu

All day long, playing on the surf,
Like those waves keeping time
With your dance.

Crocheted bikini with a head full of sand.
Seashell smiles in your eyes
Upon your Strawberry Moon Face.

Who would dare deny you
Every pleasure of the flesh
While your hair is always on fire?

Life keeps you moving
To a pace unlike the ocean
On the Eastern shores.

But I see you in Malibu,
Wild and alone.
Soul laughing at the sun.

I'll meet you there.
Peaceful waters of the western front
Will bear witness to our return.

The Moon is a Harlot

I sing of torture, blissed.
Struggle, sand and surf tryst.

My heart is open
To the flow of the ocean,
My shores barren sand
Beaten stones into land.

Every wave a lover
Breaking against one another.

Cursed Moon and your power,
Rule desire and tidal hour.
Drags attention from the beach,
Wanton waters ache to reach.

Leaving parched my skin
And untouched within.

With your wiles of light,
In the orb of the night;
Deceptive mistress of the surf,
No copulations, no birth.

Darkness enlightens your form,
But from this no love is born.

Then your wave
Washed resolve I gave.
I want your wave to stay,
No Moon draws you away.

Swell and ripple upon me
With your surging sea.

Where your breakers crashed
Left me unabashed.
Clean in baptism,
Rinsed of skepticism.

If you linger on my shore,
Perhaps I will love once more.

For that mistress misleads,
All shine with no deeds.
A tease, you find all too soon;
You cannot touch the Moon.

The Duke

Sensitive and blessed,
A well-loved boy, raised up
Tickling keys of pianos
And attentions of young ladies.

Pool hall minority
And burlesque theaters,
Juvenescent curtain exposed
Education Mother wouldn't imagine.

High society of the capital
Begged a sound below
What an aristocratic ear
Could feel and hear.

Harlem's promise beckoned
With no mention of the struggle.
Dreams blended into music,
Realized in the Cotton Club.

Sweet, bawdy tones.
Engage bodies, long and lean,
Encouraged the stomping sway
From handsome fingers.

Sophisticated Mr. Ellington.
Master of tactual rhapsody.
Elegance strived to achieve
What the Duke owned.

M.E.W.
(Mistrust in the Eyes of a Woman)

Cats don't care for poetry.
They don't want your words.
Neither do I.

I want your loving tone.
Your hands, stroking.
Your eyes, smiling.

Creatures know lies.
Unable to be told.
Deeds are the undoing.

There's cat hair
Sticking to everything.
Dull reminders of deceit.

I love my cat.
For me,
He has no words.

Mew.

Caffe Kilim

Sleigh bells herald the entry
Caffeine deprived bourgeois folk.
Evil eyes repel
And Yalcin's thick voice embraces.

From dream into steamy bean,
Cream clouds arouse.
Sugar slides,
Sweet sandy sludge.

Turkish textiles,
Worldly postcards advertise
Exotic outposts exclaiming:
"Wish You Were Here".

They are sent here
To live among the wall art.
Pillow laden benches
Dripping in Anatolian flare.

Confections and edible delights
Accompany hookahs,
Muslim crescent and star
And Christmas lights.

You are very welcome.
Global orchestras throb,
Beckoning you to partake
In the Dancing Goats.

Alexandria: Hypatia's Passion

Great son of the God of gods
And Macedonian Queen,
Conquered and gave his name
To legend of cities mastered.

As it was in Pharaoh's land
Where Persians had subdued,
Egyptian unified with Greek
Under Alexander's love.

In triumph grew a causeway,
Gateway to the grand harbor.
Bathed in a glow of safety
By the wonder of the ancient lighthouse.

True illumination came forth
From origin of thought.
Her library possessed
Municipal pride and Hypatia's passion.

Wealth of wisdom gathered
From ancient world, this urban port
Collected scientists, scribes, minds
And papyrus.

These precious gems,
Largest stores of knowledge,
Lost to pillage and rape.
Her blessings burned, lost to time.

Linger with Me

That soft spot, the hollow
Near your throbbing intent,
Begs my lips
To kiss.

Were I to fold, to give
To the want I bear
And the ache you harbor,
We could eagerly lay in content.

Ah, but to taunt myself
And to tease you,
Would it not allow
Our delight to ignite?

I want a slow burn, with you.
The ash of a fast-flash of flame
Cannot remain.
And I want to stay.

For the moment, just this moment
I refrain from the kiss.
Bliss-twisted breath
After the lightest of lick.

Love for Joni's Palette

Tired soles of your cowgirl boots
Carried you to California,
Celtic Eskimo lady.
Call of the snowbird, wanderlust-
You flew on to see.
Aching artist yearning.
That town, that taste, that man.
Travelers touching briefly
Forge bonds of precious value.
Wine of tragic romantic tales,
This sweet Canadian gypsy
Drinking in the drowning.
Seaside Viking cries of tides,
Women waiting, wailing,
Souls worn thin by the coast.
Encamped in humble charity
Pilgrims fall together.
Kinship of the hobo's creed signed by
Flaxen haired goddess of song.
Heart dripping in paint and pain,
Moving on to another cabaret.
Her siren song calling
Another drifter to join the pavement.
Heartbroken hitchhiker,
She cries when he's gone
And leaves when the North wind blows cold.
Looking for that river.
Sharpening her skates.
Really, she's just a painter
Haunted by her canvas.
Seeking the next empty frame.

Orion

Osiris will return someday.
Restored, resting in the womb
Of the night sky's hunter.
Birthplace of stars, of us,
Of knowledge advanced.
Given to ancestors
Comprised of celestial dust,
As we, grasping, aching,
For a place in the cerebral nebula.
Worshipped across oceans
And ages of time,
This warrior's belt
Immortalized in shrines.
Cave impressions of stars
Both Hopi and Nubian,
Megalithic monument
Of Mayan and Pharaoh,
To mysteries of Sumerian carvings.
Possessed astral answers
Given by those "gods".
Misplaced by the civilized,
Reclaimed by sands of time.
What judgment does he pass
Upon us from his lofty throne?
Oh how these ancient secrets
Pervert contemporary beliefs.
Our wisdom is primitive.

Ballad of Anne Boleyn (part 1)

In the countryside of Kent
A maiden born of privilege,
Education and finery.
Armed with fertile mind,
Welcoming demeanor
And bewitching gaze,
She came to Hampton Court.
Schooled as a lady-in-waiting,
The complexity of a French kiss
Imprinted upon her.
Wooing those who dared
To breathe the sensual essence
Of this plain faced lady.
Capturing the affections of poet Wyatt
And the heart of a Tudor king,
Having not a noble look
But an essence of knowing desire.
A siren at the art of passion
And her own limitations.
Treachery lies in speaking grace
To a woman who wears a mask,
Not so fair
But possessing an air
Of a wanton, well cherished bedchamber.
Revealing beauty to this mistress
Is akin to confessing pure love.
Most dangerous of games.

Ballad of Anne Boleyn (part 2)

Lighting a flame
Beneath a phoenix
Hastened this poor bird
Succumb to aroused combustion.
Force a regal hand
Of an iron man
Into a hound's paw.
Gave a golden whistle
To this bitch,
License to blow
And call this sovereign cur.
This mistress stands firm.
Her ground is virtue,
Maddening her liege.
And with a barren queen
To give no heir.
A Great Matter,
An impending empty throne.
Takes her as his own,
Scorned wife in dispose.
Marquess then consort
Of the crown.
Britannia quaked
And her church exiled.
Reformation for love,
One thousand day's reign
With no prince,
Sever her head from heart.

Daybreak

Dare I attempt to capture
The rapture my soul found
In the painting of the morning sky?

Indigo amethyst assault
Upon the velvet black,
Carnal fingers caressing arousal.

Dazzling scandal of violent red,
Ripped open.
Bleeds gashes of orange rage.

Heeded warning.
Wise sailor who rises
For the spectacle of prediction.

Vermillion bashful turns to blush
With the rising of the charming sun.
Blazing lustful light through her gown.

Rouge fades, a pallid memory.
Dawn pales to a fleshy hue,
Citrine veil draped across her face.

Warmth ascends,
Pulls a blanket of joyful blue
As sun sobers the day.

Good morning.

Naughty Nymphs

Prankish pixies pounce playfully,
Traipsing teasingly through terrain.
Daring desirous dancers,
Raunchy riotous rubbings,
Lovingly licking lightly,
Torturous tickles taunt.
Pubic petals pulsing
Seize stiffening stamen spawn
Orgy of oozing orgasmic offerings,
Fornicating freely for flowers.
Delightedly drinking down
Visions of visceral view.
Impetuous imps in intimate indulgence,
Later lay lazily lounging
Under umbrellas of undergrowth.
Dozing drifting dreamless of
Erotic elves entangled excess.
Naughty nymphs nuzzle nightly
For fertile fascination of forests.

Earthly Delights in the Dirt

If my ears could hear the sound
Of fertile seeds breaking ground
Would I recognize the music it would make?

If my eyes could drink the sight
Of deepest greens in moonlight
Could I trust my mind to truly see?

If this flower has scent to savor
Of the sweetness taste the flavor
Should I dare to do so w/ my tongue?

If my garden yields to rain
Of the harsh and driving pain
Shall I venture in to feel it on my skin?

All Cycle and Dance

Find a life of cultivation,
Nurturing terra and turf.
Strawberries eager welcome summer
And attentions of your kitchen.

Beans and peas
Strive sunward through their tripods,
Twisting ascending begging
Sweet kisses from Apollo.

Soil bound roots
Seek comfort in the womb-like throbbing.
Summer's heat conceives bounty.
True gift when breaking ground.

The Winter's bleakness blankets.
Renders rest upon the weak terrain.
This embryonic sleep
Guarded by Orion, night watchman.

The seemingly dormant seeds
Spring, bring to chance.
Love, dirt, hands
All cycle and dance.

Merely a Meal

Trifecta of taste
Celery, carrot and onion.
Simple saute sweats,
Steam permeates pores.

Garlic argues with
The sweet dancers sway,
Turns to sultry samba.
Jealous pungent punch of musk.

Abused fruit chaos,
Burst of sanguine tomato.
Burgundy infuses,
Cheered by sweet basil.

Slow low heat.
Flavor tango tempered,
Simmer and stew,
Left to lusty embrace.

Violent boiling begs
Noodly attentions.
Once brittle and stubborn,
Concedes to submissive frailty.

Tart teasing cheese,
Parmesan tickles
Saucy aggressive gravy
Blankets shy penne.

Sown Seeds of Scion

Weary wet wanton wells
Passion pit of perilous pulsing
Desire denied driving deed
Fueling fire forces fits of fury
Root and ripen riots rapture
Within walls of weakened womb.
Forsaken fornication frustrated fuse
Begs bonds of bliss.
Urges unrequited under unison
Anarchic ache aims artful arrows
Spearing shaft soliciting smut
Wreaking worship of warm wickedness
Damp domain dried debauchery
Sticky syrup surplus sentiment
Achieves amorous absorption
Moaning memories mope, muddied marination
Copulation cradled, cooing contentment.
Brazen bud brings branch to bough.

Early Autumn Came the Fall

Bright bouquets of leaves.
Young trees in a grove,
Caught my gaze early this autumn.

In my daily travels
These fleeting images
Hastily taken for granted.

The camera lens can wait.
Another day, another time...
When I can find it.

You left us on a Friday.

I had waited too long.
On my path the leaves were gone.
That picture, never taken.

For Us (part 1)

Cold surrounds, lost in the sunlit stories played out
By frost on the window, an inch from my cheek.
Swaying along rails leading far from the cities,
To mountainous regions, we flee to seek...

Isolation so pure. Ours.
Hours upon hours of travelling time.
Landscapes of patchwork designs to find
A quiet bliss so sublime.

I breathe, a chance to alter
The scene alight, icy dancers on glass.
To melt and reveal a world alive!
But unknown by those in first class.

Deep shadows of life tremble and scatter
With the oncoming of the massive, steaming beast.
Our chariot cuts through days, nights, fields of snow,
All food for thought for us to feast.

Which is all merely a simple backdrop
For us, those lovers in the last car, alone.
Destined for lost countryside to house
A good man and woman, a pauper's throne.

For Us (part 2)

Morning crisp, awake and depart.
Station, shuffling of strangers, shy snowflakes land.
Our carriage awaits us impatiently now,
As my attentions, held in your hand.

Warm embraces, spaces held within
Soft lamplight, curtains enclosed surround.
You're taking me while losing furs,
Quiet horse hooves and bells sound.

Taste. Touching tortured flesh
Of sweet, sweat-infused need.
Softness taken in enflamed starvation,
As soil aches for a seed.

Swiftly passing through hands over hours,
And hands slowly passing over skin.
Miles slide as we, hidden together,
Approach divine unity within.

As our lust-encompassed coach slows,
To our view, a scene enchanted.
Wood smoke perfumed palace peace,
For us, a shared wish granted.

Curtains

Tortured textiles descend
From the ceiling to the floor.
Hanging heavy in my mind
I can't cry anymore.

Lost are the blues & deeper reds,
Purples lack of sin;
Jewels fallen from their threads,
The silvers pale to tin.

Faded from time,
And forgotten like vow;
These curtains
Block the sunlight now.

Taking down the fabric
That to weave was a trial.
Bright tapestries ahead of me,
In this I find a smile.

I once found great joy
In mere thought of what we'd weave;
Together, and what we would create!
Our life we would conceive!

Your stitches make no sense to me,
And the choice of color and where.
I choose now to sew alone,
And I wish I didn't care.

Cold Sun

Golden glow,
Fights against the grey gloom.
Gives way and fades.
Mood most valiant a foe to light.

I want to bask.
Exposed, absorbing glory.
Warm winds of August encourage
Tear-like sweat and rapture.

Raise my temperament
As mercury dances higher.
Rays blinding with renewal.
Spirit bathed by baptismal dawn.

Month of my birth begs
Embrace, denied by this cold sun.
My January stands bereft,
Hardened heart of bitter hurt.

These polar days of winter
Bite and punish
Those who dare
To endure the distress.

Mocked by mildly glowing orb,
A mere specter of itself.
Lovers mistaken as siblings,
So similar, sun and moon.

Days of glacial doom
Be damned.
Grant me the sight of beauty
In cruel mornings, fading into twilight.

Siberian madness,
Snow abusing sanctity.
Slowly overtakes reason,
Slicing through sanity.

All is needed in one moment.
Clarity, crispness of air.
Delicacy of hoarfrost,
Delivery in delight from the ice.

We will see this fade into spring.
Haze of the hungry mind
Shrouded, once more will feel
Aroused by the tickle of May.

Only in These Short Hours

Late night liquor.
Spiced singed tongue of smoky scorched leaf.
Lied to you. I care.
But only in these short hours dare to admit.

Cold early autumn days
Cut my resolve.
To know you now
Is like visiting a ghost.

I know you care, too.
Your barbaric cheap beer
And long, tortured drags of your cigarette.
And me, haunting your head.

Only in these short hours...

Seacoast Salutes Spring

Barren black branches
Grasping grieving gold.
Long lifeless limbs
Against the aggressive Atlantic,
Beaten by blustery blows.
Flashes of finches,
Choreography of cardinals cavorting,
Winter wrens waging war
With western winds.
Sweet scent of soil
Sneaks silently
Through the trapped tundra.
Frost fondles freely,
Sun sentenced in slavery.
Chains conquered,
Gilded glimmer glare
Bringing bud to birth,
Blush bursting into bloom.
Grief of grass a ghost
Exorcised in easy emergence.
Dawn delight draws deep.
Crocus creep cautiously
Fear-filled for freeze,
Yet yielding to yawning youth.
Winning, waking warmth within.
Sobbing Springtime sighs into
Puddles, plight of precipitation
Crying cheerful chorus,
Liberates lifeless landscape.

Zenith of Mr. Frost

Walking these roads
Steps being choices
Made well in momentary
Placement of one's footfall
On cobblestones.
Or on asphalt, or dirt,
Perhaps found in a yellow wood.
Standing at the crossroad
Failing to find favor
In one way or another.

Equally worn routes,
But mine was less traveled still.
I never realized
Until now, the zenith
Of this moment here
And in my choosing
Elected to walk away.

Chase Me To Paris

Chase me to Paris,
I have so much to say;
All I have to use
Are words.

I need an act of divination.
More than words.
Some truth
That cannot be swallowed.

No drink of port wine
Nor bitter pill,
Powder, puff of smoke
Or Dionysian dream can awaken.

Lights of the City
Illuminating what needs to be seen.
There must be some raw honesty
In some corner, waiting for me.

So, chase me to Paris.
Laughing and racing through the streets.
Tragic romance of historic cobblestones
Entering our pores.

Centaurs and Metaphors

Possessed with barbaric drive.
Untamed racing;
Majestic, animalistic, chaotic,
Throwing my words down as they form.

Unbridled man,
My language runs amuck.

I struggle to harness and ride,
Guide these wild notions.
Domesticate these beasts within,
Civilize the centaur.

This creature
Is my poetic ego.

The human subdues
The feral horse of a mind.
Takes the reins
And rides the stanza home.

Perverted cousins from gods,
Hybrids of what we are and want to be.

My thoughts are savage,
Tamed by the mortal.
The man-beast refines
And sophisticates into verse.

Oyster River

On a tiny island
There's a tattered sign
And the words have worn away.

Lost.
How many words have been lost?

About the Author

Being moved by image provoking writing all her life, Claire Conroy has always felt connected to words and the effects they have on people. One of many varied interests, writing has been revisited throughout her life. During an especially difficult break up years ago, poetry became a valued outlet for healing. She decided to start the project she has always longed to achieve, to finally write a volume of poetry. Claire realized all her experiences up to that point was to get to this precipice and take that final leap into the literary world.

Late nights of dedicated soul diving, anguish and enthusiasm, she has compiled over 40 poems. Musings on heartbreak, love and passion; appreciation and worship of life and nature; praising and damning of historical figures and funny observations from the emotional emancipation of a 40-something year old woman from Portsmouth, NH.